THE SEASHORE

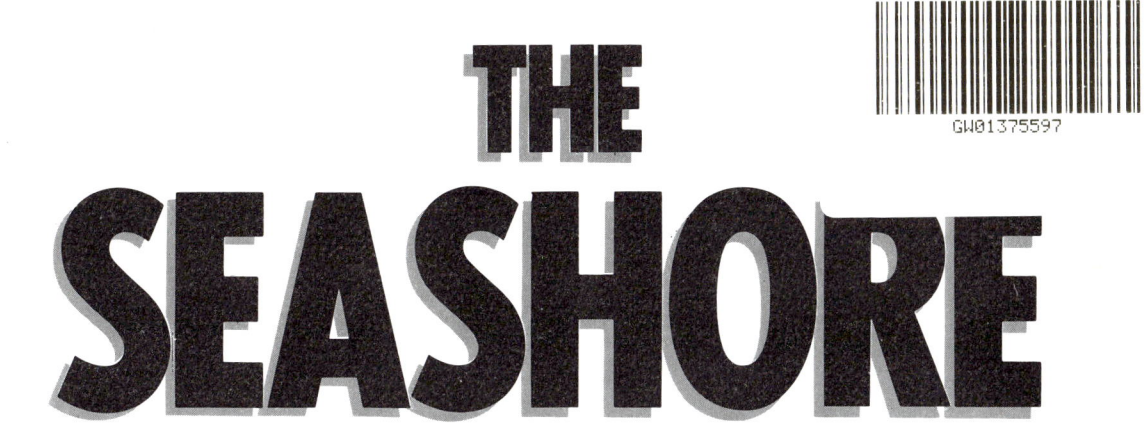

Sea Cliffs 2
Sandy Shores 8
Rocks and Shingle 14
In the Rock Pool 20

Kingfisher Books

Sea Cliffs

Although the cliff face looks like a rocky and uncomfortable place to live, it provides an excellent breeding ground for seabirds. High up on cliff ledges, the birds can build their nests and raise their young without being in danger from hunters such as stoats, rats and foxes.

Seabirds nest in huge groups, called colonies. The breeding area is busy and noisy, since the birds are always squabbling amongst themselves over space on the narrow ledges.

It is more difficult for plants to survive on the steep cliffs, because there is little soil for them to take root in. You will see far more plants on sloping cliffs, which are made of softer rocks such as clay.

Always take great care near cliffs, and never go near the edge. It is much safer to look at them from below.

Herring Gull (56–66 cm). This gull is a familiar sight at the seashore, with its grey body, yellow beak and pink legs. It soars high overhead on powerful black-tipped wings, and feeds on the shellfish that live on the shoreline. Gulls will also take food from rubbish tips, and can often be seen following fishing boats in search of scraps.

Puffin (30 cm). A small plump seabird that breeds in burrows at the top of cliffs. Its body is black and white, and the most striking feature is the colourful, parrot-like beak. It has orange legs and webbed feet, which help it to swim underwater.

Gannet (85–100 cm). These large seabirds are always exciting to watch, as they glide on the air currents and dive steeply into the sea to catch fish in their strong beaks. Their wings are long, straight and pointed, and beat stiffly in flight.

Thrift (up to 15 cm). Thrift is also called Sea Pink, and it makes a pretty splash of colour on the rocks and cliffs where it blooms between April and August. It has sturdy stems, and a thick cushion of leaves which help to protect it from strong sea breezes.

Sea Buckthorn (up to 3 metres). This large shrub grows well on cliffs and dunes. It has brown, thorny twigs, which put out silvery leaves. Its tiny green flowers open in March and April, and its orange berries help to brighten up the coastline in the winter months.

Sea Mayweed (up to 70 cm). A type of daisy, found on cliffs and dunes as well as in fields near the sea. The flowers have a yellow centre, with many white petals. The leaves are narrow and fleshy, with feathery leaflets.

Rock Samphire (15–30 cm) is a cliffside plant with many branches and a woody stem. The tiny, yellowish flowers appear from mid-summer until the end of August, and form umbrella-shaped flower-heads at the end of the stems. The leaves are smooth and fleshy, and are divided into narrow sections.

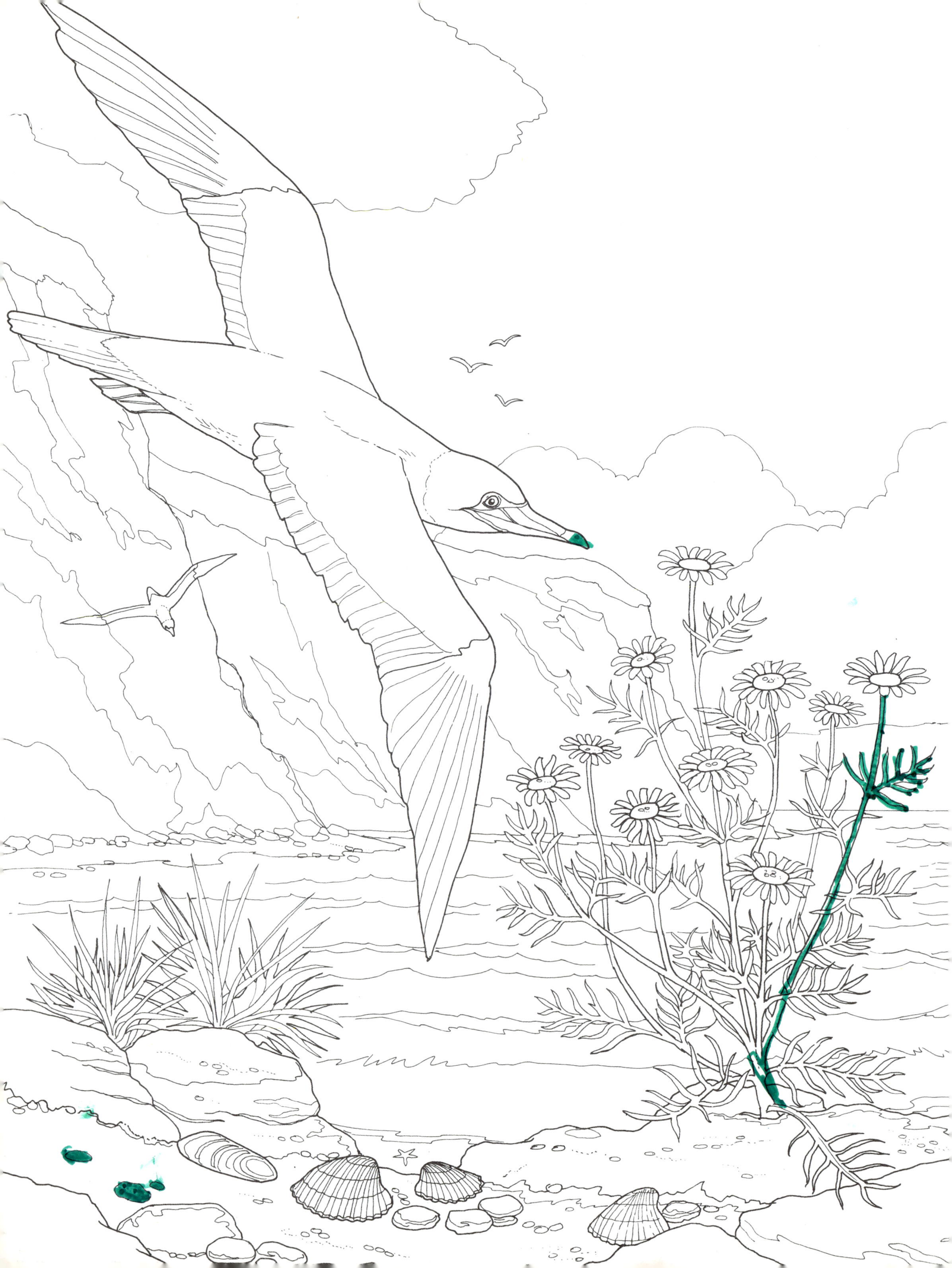

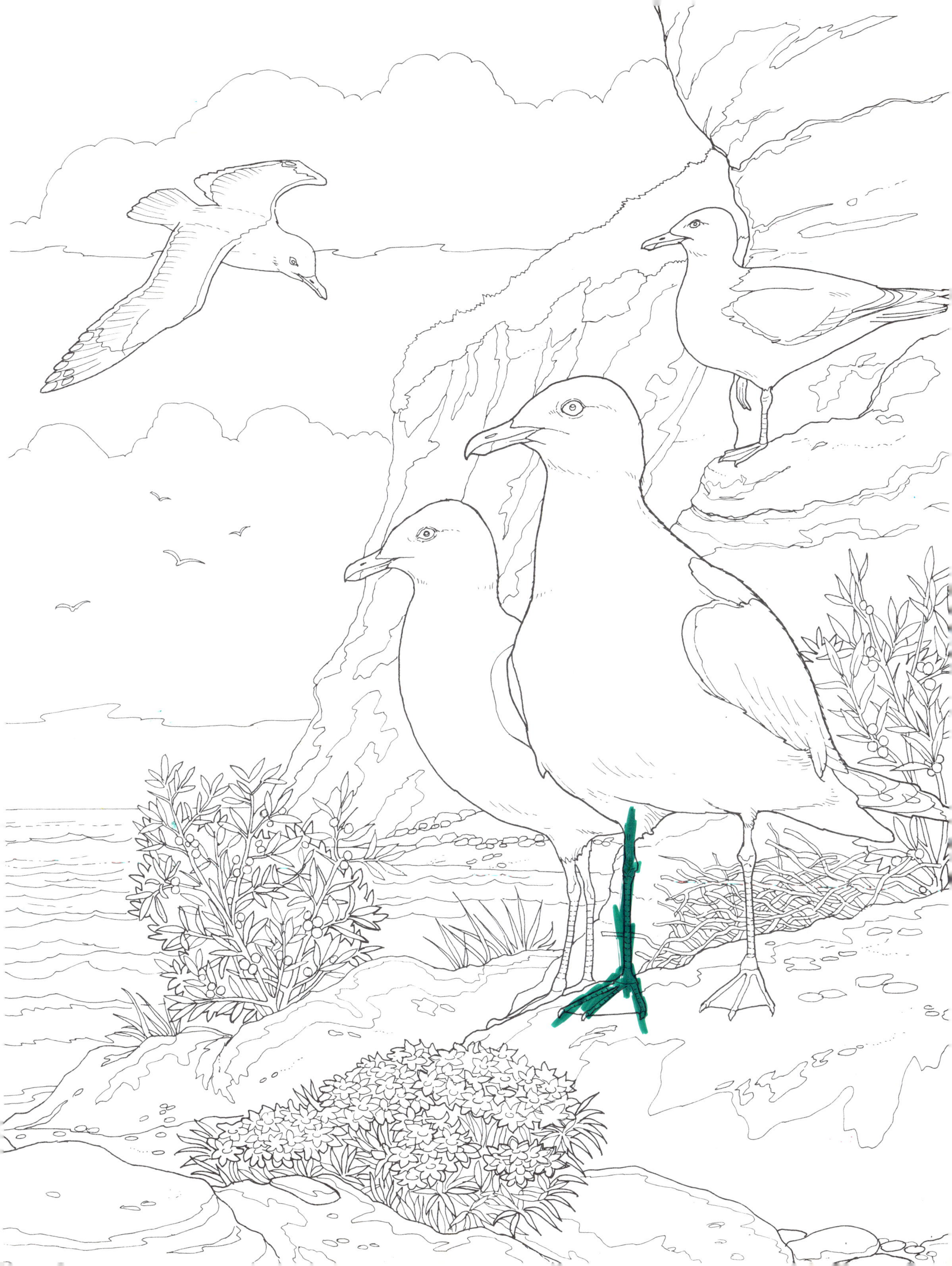

Sandy Shores

Sand is made up of tiny pieces of rock and shell, which have been ground down over thousands of years by the waves pounding on the shore. In some places, the wind piles the sand up into ridges called dunes. Since these are above the high-water line, plants can grow there without being disturbed by the sea. The roots of the plants reach down into the sand in search of water, and stop the dunes from being shifted about by the sea breezes.

When the tide goes out, the sand looks deserted. But there is plenty of life just under the surface. Many small, burrowing creatures hide here at low tide, safe from the seabirds that wheel overhead. When the sand is covered by water again, these animals come out to feed on the plants and pieces of dead fish that are swept in by the sea. The waves also wash up seaweed and shells, and you may even find the remains of jellyfish along the tide line.

Sea Bindweed (about 5 cm) is one of the prettiest plants on the shoreline. It is usually found on sand dunes, where the long creeping stems help to stop the sand from blowing away. The heart-shaped leaves are bright green, and the trumpet-like flowers have pale pink and purple petals. These appear in summer and early autumn.

Sea Holly (30–60 cm). Sea Holly is a tall and spiky plant which grows on sand and shingle beaches. The whole plant is pale blue in colour. At the top of the stem are the prickly blue flowerheads, which appear between July and August. The spiny blue-green leaves have white veins, and are covered with a waxy coat.

Ringed Plover (19 cm). The Ringed Plover is easy to spot, with its striped brown wings, black collar and black tip at the end of a short yellow bill. It nests on the ground, and uses a clever trick to protect its young from enemies. If a fox shows interest in the nest, the Plover will lure it away by pretending to have a broken wing. The fox thinks it has found an easy meal, until the Plover flies safely away again!

Lugworm (up to 20 cm). All that is usually seen of the Lugworm is its cast. This is the small coil of sand that the worm leaves behind it on the surface, as it burrows down in search of food and shelter. Its body is thick and round, becoming thinner at the tail. The bright red gills on its body are used for breathing.

Masked Crab (up to 5 cm). Even when this small yellow crab is hiding beneath the surface, you may see the tips of its hairy antennae poking up above the sand at low tide. Its long, narrow shell has spines on each side, and the male crab's legs are twice as long as its body. The female has shorter legs.

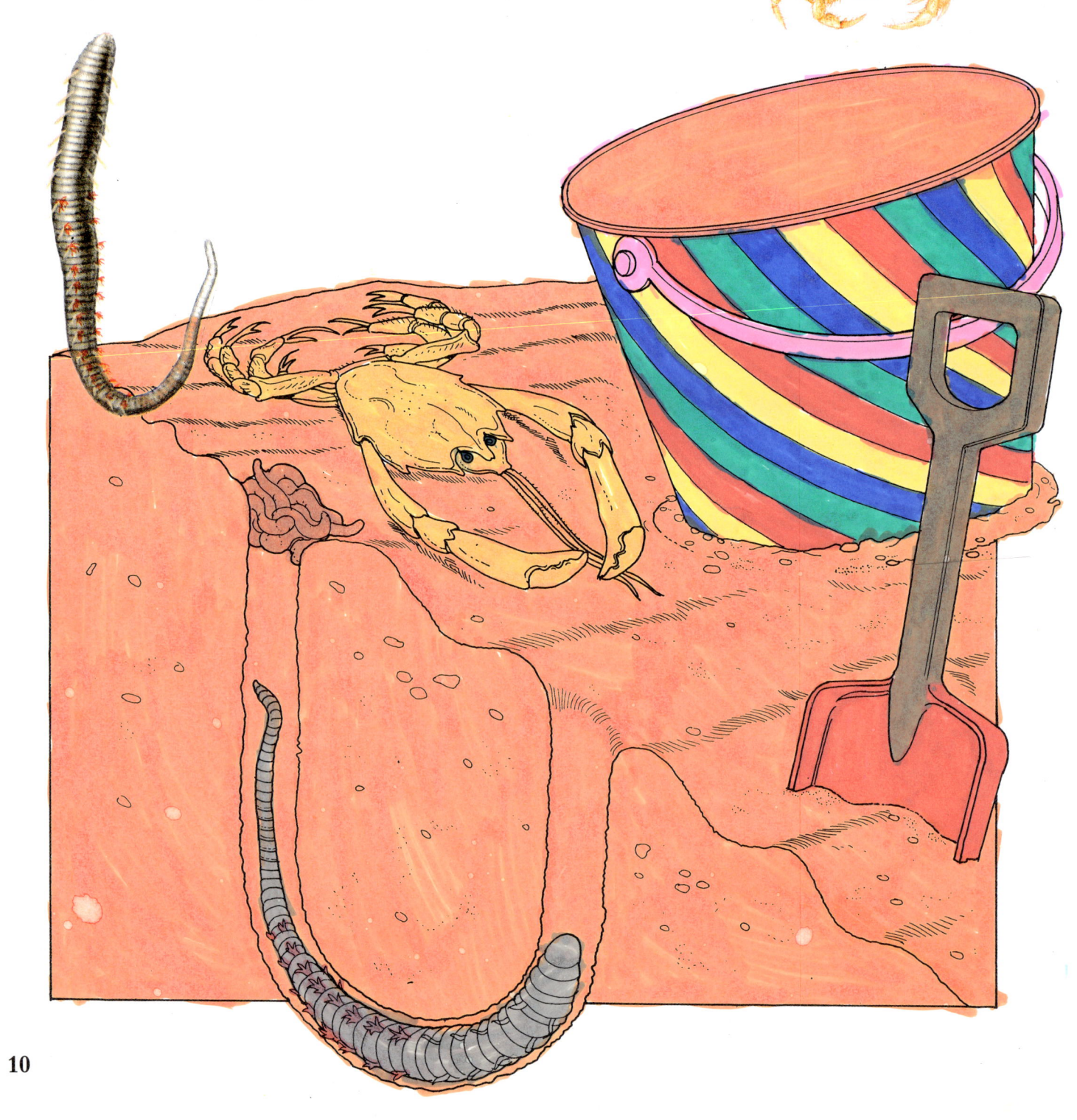

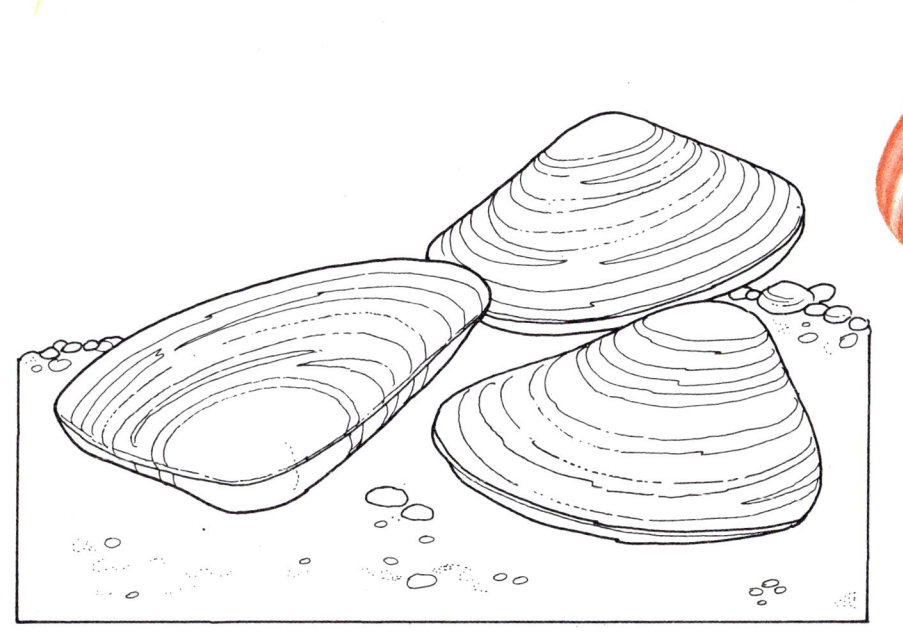

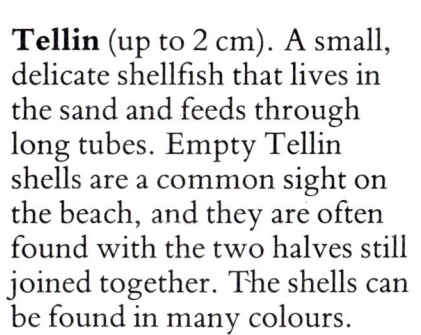

Tellin (up to 2 cm). A small, delicate shellfish that lives in the sand and feeds through long tubes. Empty Tellin shells are a common sight on the beach, and they are often found with the two halves still joined together. The shells can be found in many colours.

Sand Mason (up to 30 cm). Much of this worm's body is covered by a long, crusty tube. It makes the tube itself, by sticking together pieces of sand and shell. The thicker front part of the worm has tufts of red gills and a mass of pale pink tentacles, which it waves above the sand in search of food at low tide.

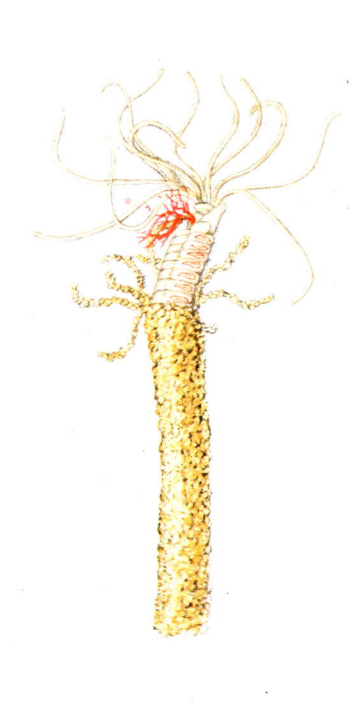

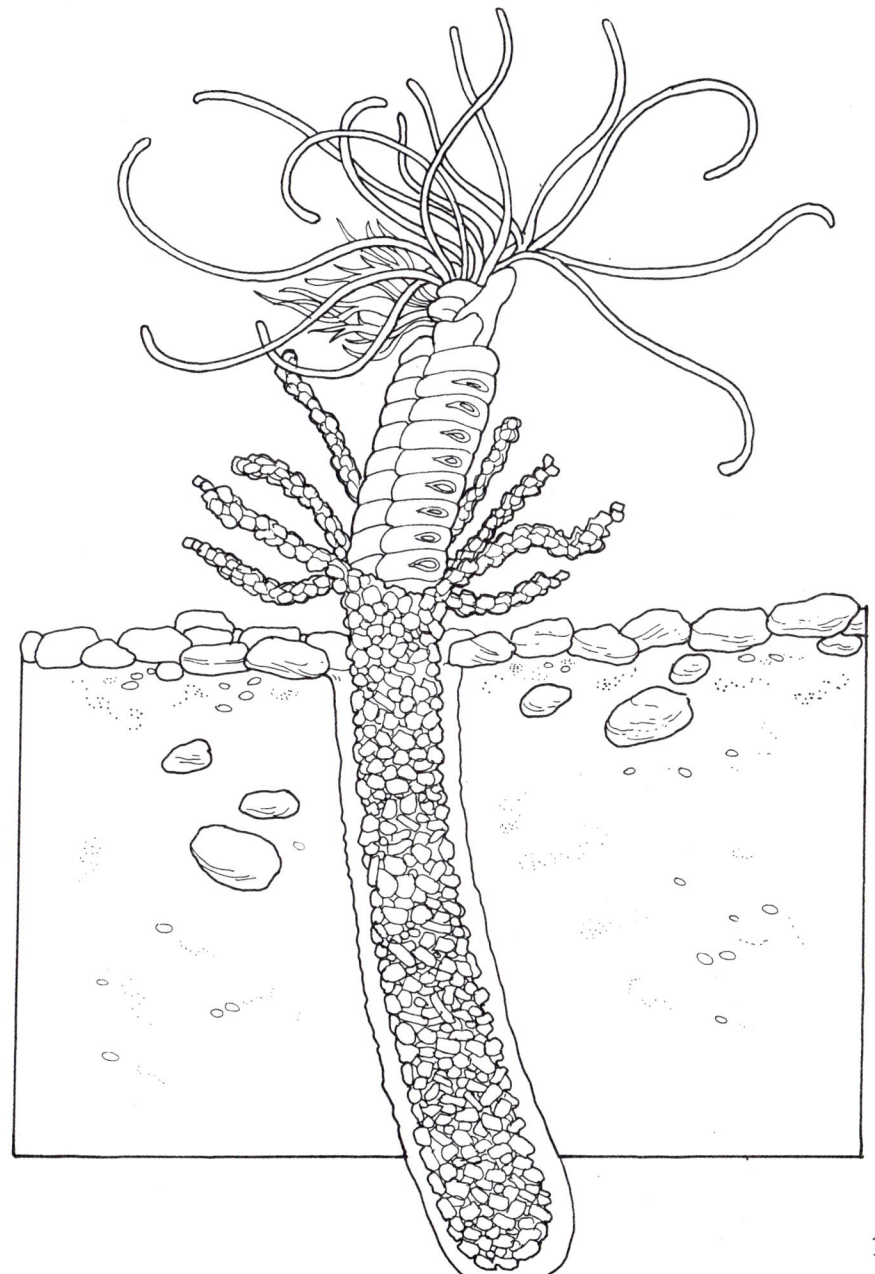

Moon Jelly (up to 20 cm). This jellyfish is often stranded on the beach by the tide. It is shaped like a tiny umbrella, with stinging tentacles around its rim. Four larger tentacles dangle underneath, and are used to push food into the jellyfish's mouth. The Moon Jelly is transparent, with pale blue and purple markings.

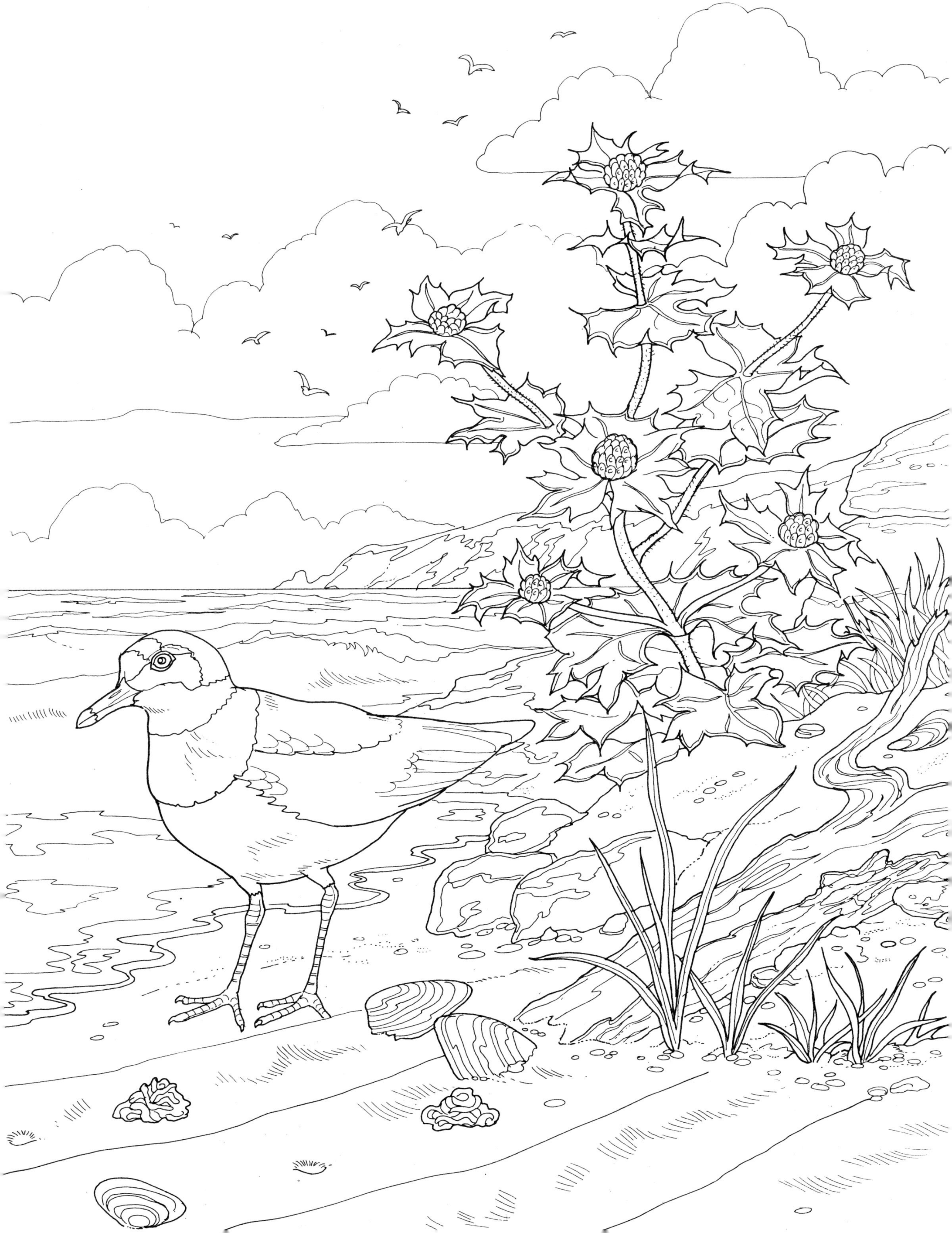

Rocks and Shingle

Like the animals that make their homes on sandy beaches, the creatures living on rocky shores have to survive the pounding of the sea twice a day. When they are not being swamped by salty water, they are left high and dry at the mercy of the sun and wind. Yet a great number of plants and animals do manage to survive here. Many animals have tough outer shells that stop them from drying out at low tide, and which also help to protect them from birds. Seaweeds have strong roots that anchor them to the rocks, and fronds which can sway with the waves without breaking when the tide comes in. On shingly beaches, plants can grow above the high-water level by sending down long roots to find water. They also have thick, fleshy leaves to stop them drying out in sunny weather.

The shore is also a good feeding ground for seabirds. They often have long, probing beaks which help them to pick out the small animals and insects that hide beneath damp clumps of seaweed or under stones.

Oystercatcher (42–44 cm). The loud, piping call of the Oystercatcher can often be heard around rocky shores. It is a striking bird, with glossy black and white feathers and a bright orange bill. Because the bill is very strong, it is ideal for prising open the cockles and mussels that make up its main food. Oystercatchers often roost in large flocks on the shore, with all the birds facing in the same direction.

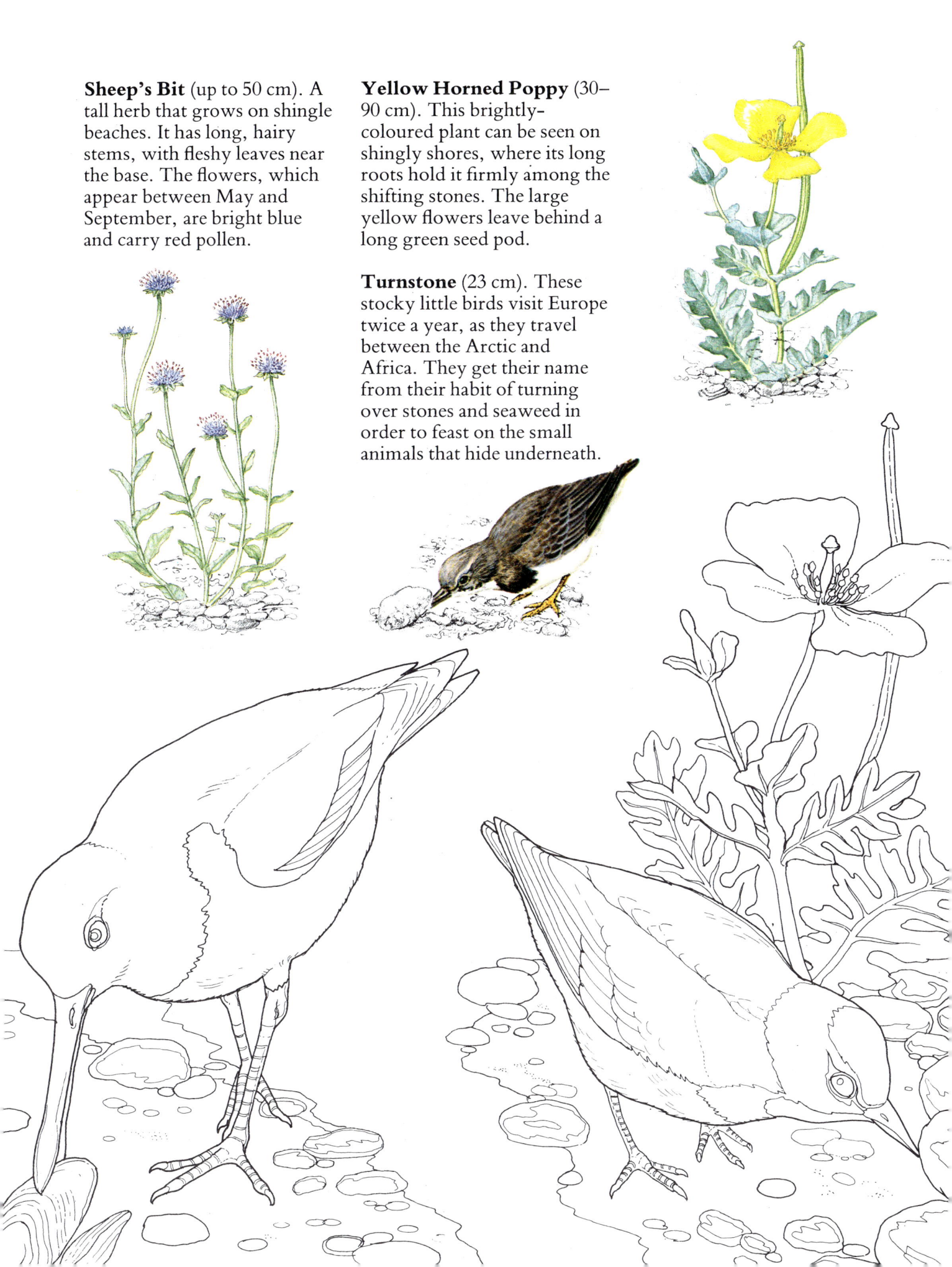

Sheep's Bit (up to 50 cm). A tall herb that grows on shingle beaches. It has long, hairy stems, with fleshy leaves near the base. The flowers, which appear between May and September, are bright blue and carry red pollen.

Yellow Horned Poppy (30–90 cm). This brightly-coloured plant can be seen on shingly shores, where its long roots hold it firmly among the shifting stones. The large yellow flowers leave behind a long green seed pod.

Turnstone (23 cm). These stocky little birds visit Europe twice a year, as they travel between the Arctic and Africa. They get their name from their habit of turning over stones and seaweed in order to feast on the small animals that hide underneath.

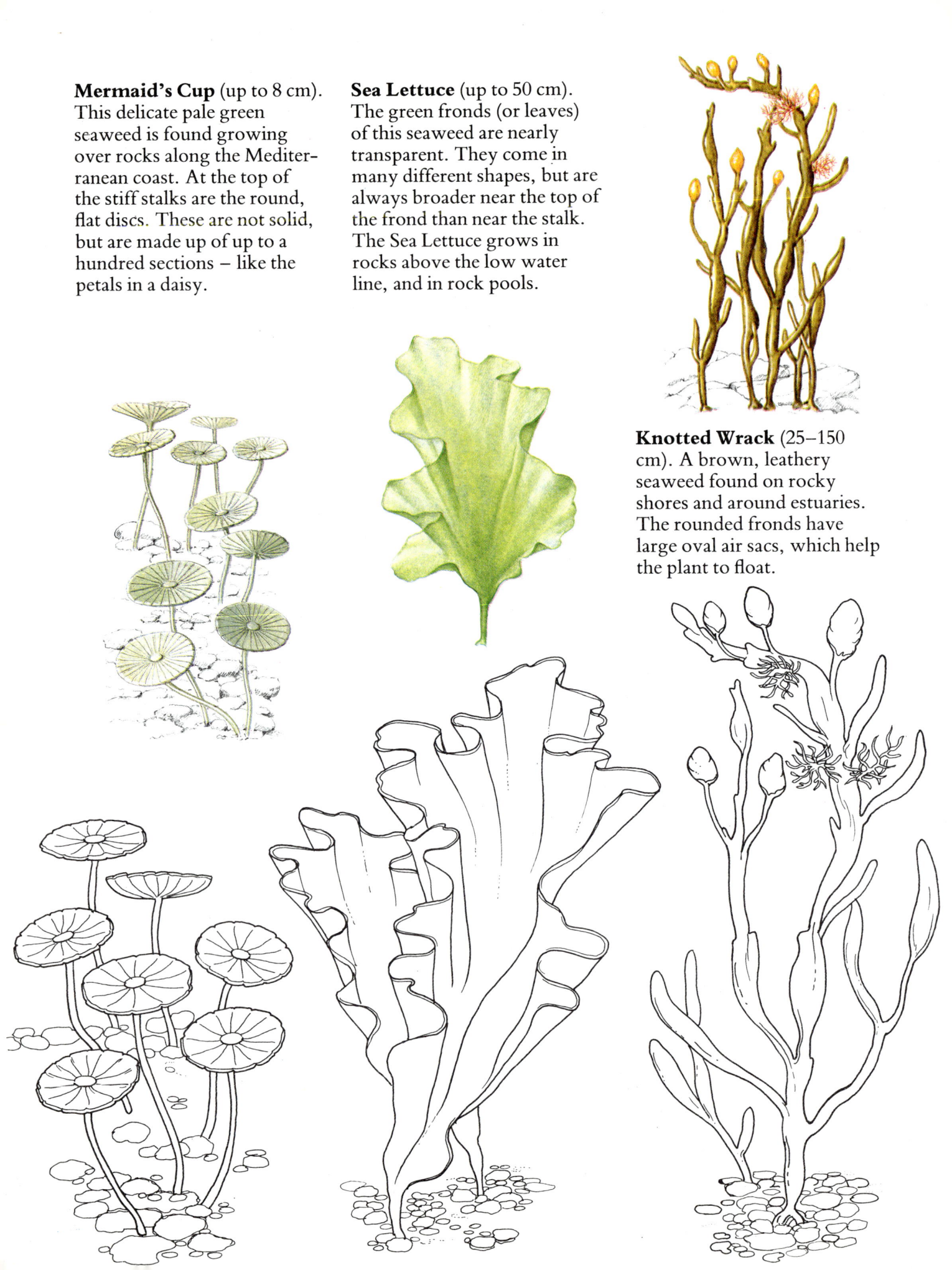

Mermaid's Cup (up to 8 cm). This delicate pale green seaweed is found growing over rocks along the Mediterranean coast. At the top of the stiff stalks are the round, flat discs. These are not solid, but are made up of up to a hundred sections – like the petals in a daisy.

Sea Lettuce (up to 50 cm). The green fronds (or leaves) of this seaweed are nearly transparent. They come in many different shapes, but are always broader near the top of the frond than near the stalk. The Sea Lettuce grows in rocks above the low water line, and in rock pools.

Knotted Wrack (25–150 cm). A brown, leathery seaweed found on rocky shores and around estuaries. The rounded fronds have large oval air sacs, which help the plant to float.

Spider Crab (up to 2 cm). This small yellow crab is often found hiding underneath fronds of seaweed. Its spider-like legs are long compared to the size of its body, which is pear-shaped and pointed at the head. The crab is often covered with small animals like sponges and worms.

Lobster (up to 50 cm). Lobsters and crabs have soft bodies, and need to grow tough outer shells to protect them. The Lobster's shell is blue-black, with red antennae. Take care if you meet one – its large front legs have powerful pincers, which can give you a nasty nip.

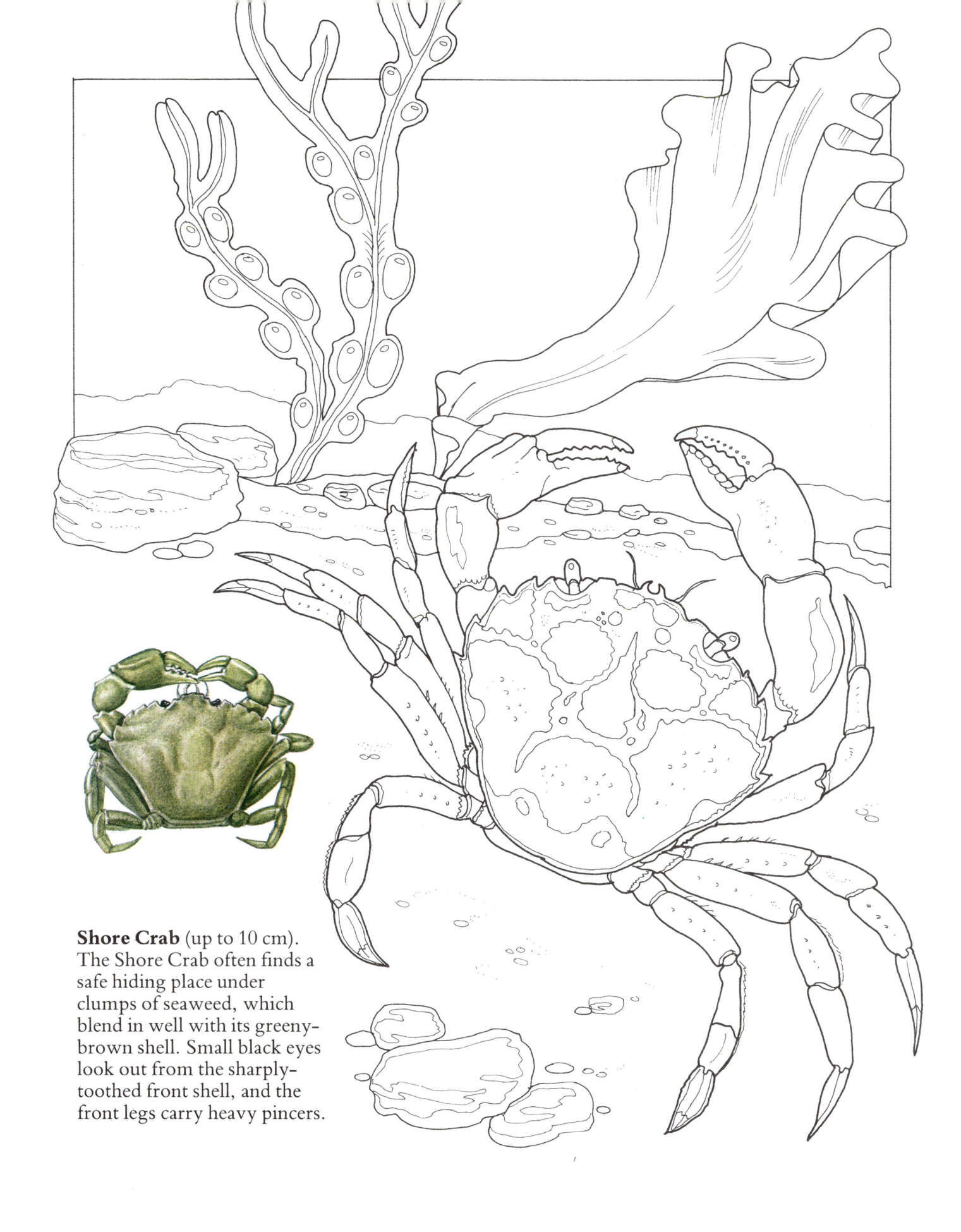

Shore Crab (up to 10 cm). The Shore Crab often finds a safe hiding place under clumps of seaweed, which blend in well with its greeny-brown shell. Small black eyes look out from the sharply-toothed front shell, and the front legs carry heavy pincers.

Edible Crab (up to 25 cm). These large orange crabs are often caught for their meat. Many live among the rocks low down on the shore, but the biggest ones are usually found in deeper water. The oval shell has a crinkled edge, and the large pincers have a black tip.

Velvet Swimming Crab (up to 12 cm). The body of the Velvet Swimming Crab is covered with fine hairs, giving it a furry look. It has bright red eyes and blue markings around the legs. It makes its home in pools and in the sea, where its flat back legs act as a paddle to help it swim.

19

In the Rock Pool

When the tide goes out, it leaves pools of water in the hollows and cracks of the rocky surface. These rock pools are the best places of all for watching seashore life in action. Try to visit the same pool at different times of the day, to see how the behaviour of the animals changes. Many of the small animals that hide under stones and seaweed when the tide has gone out become more bold when the sea washes in again. Slender fish dart through the water, in danger from the beautiful sea anemones who wave their stinging tentacles about in the hope of catching a passing meal. Crabs leave their seaweed cover to scuttle about in search of food, while shelled fish and starfish make their way more slowly over the rocks. If you watch them carefully, you can become an expert on who is hunting who in the rock pool.

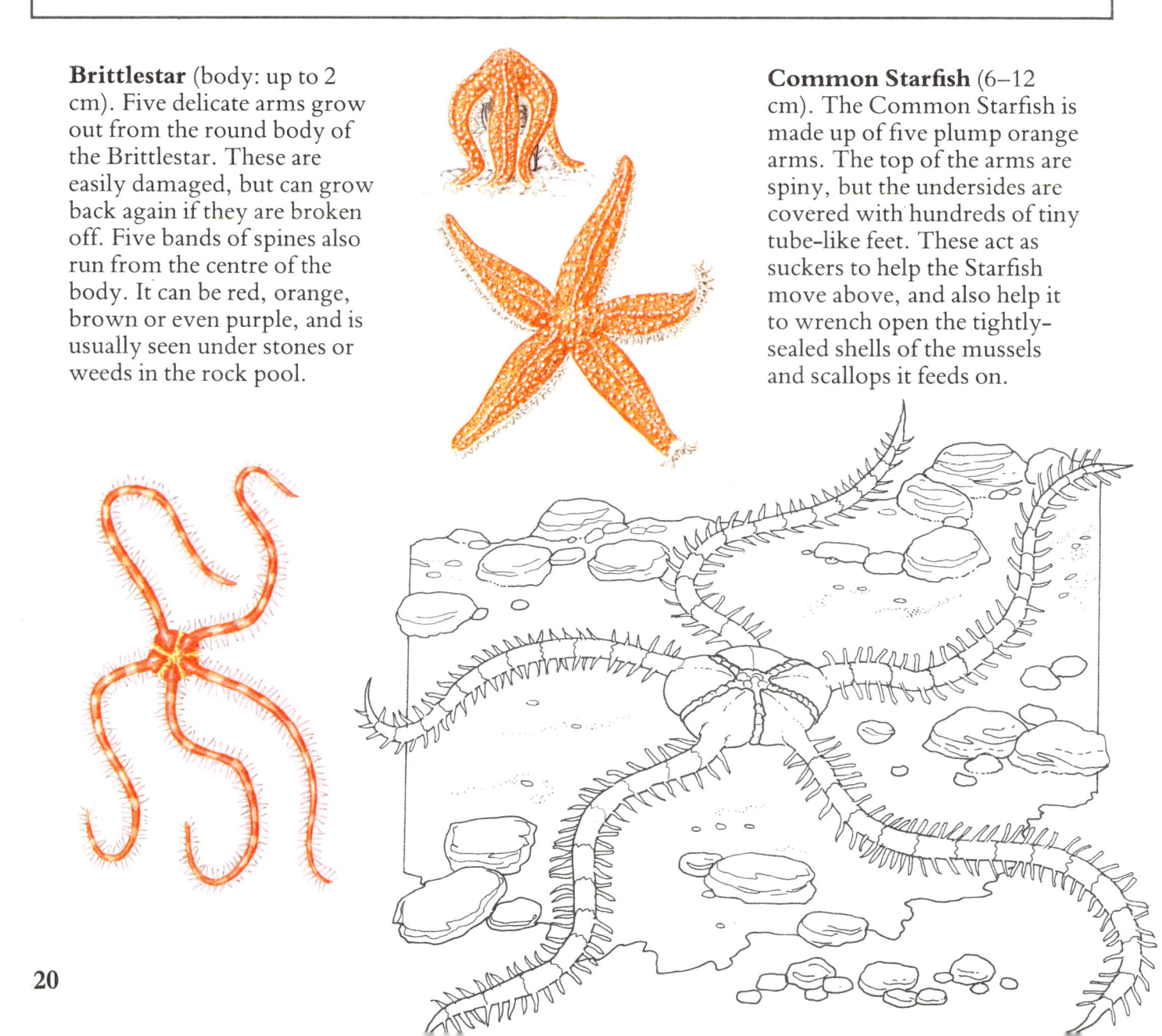

Brittlestar (body: up to 2 cm). Five delicate arms grow out from the round body of the Brittlestar. These are easily damaged, but can grow back again if they are broken off. Five bands of spines also run from the centre of the body. It can be red, orange, brown or even purple, and is usually seen under stones or weeds in the rock pool.

Common Starfish (6–12 cm). The Common Starfish is made up of five plump orange arms. The top of the arms are spiny, but the undersides are covered with hundreds of tiny tube-like feet. These act as suckers to help the Starfish move above, and also help it to wrench open the tightly-sealed shells of the mussels and scallops it feeds on.

Beadlet Anemone (up to 6 cm). When the tide is out, the Beadlet Anemone just looks like a colourful blob of jelly sticking to the side of the rockpool. But when the sea comes in again, the Anemone puts out its beautiful feeding tentacles. It waves these about in search of small animals and fish, which are then pushed into its mouth.

Snakelock Anemone (up to 15 cm). The Snakelock Anemone is larger than the Beadlet, but its body is flatter and baggier. It is often a dull brown, but can also be pink or a soft apple-green, as here. The tentacles are very long, with pale violet tips.

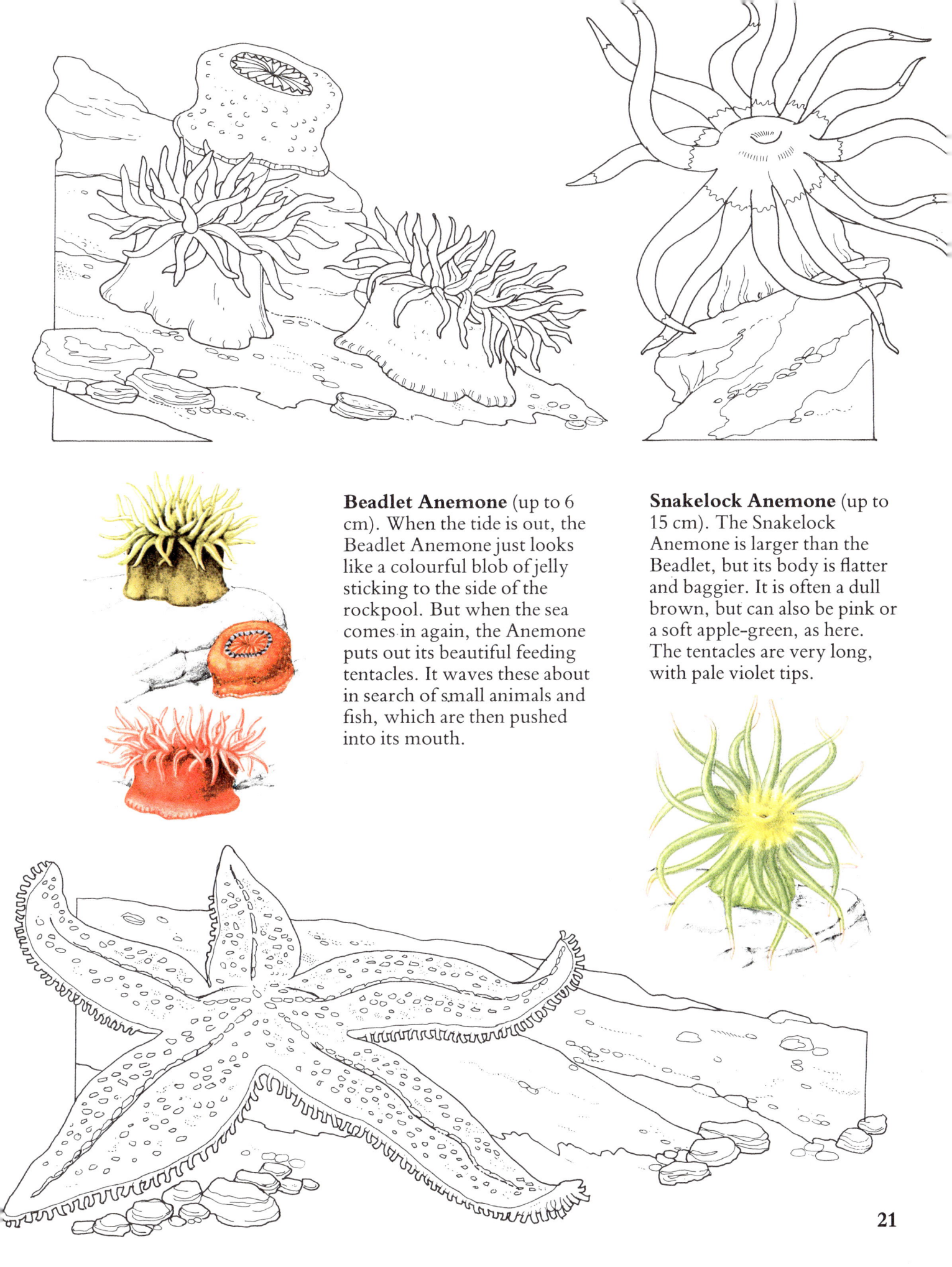

Edible Sea Urchin (up to 12 cm). This soft-bodied animal lives inside a hard, prickly shell. The empty shells can sometimes be found in rock pools, but without the pink spines that cover it when the animal is alive.

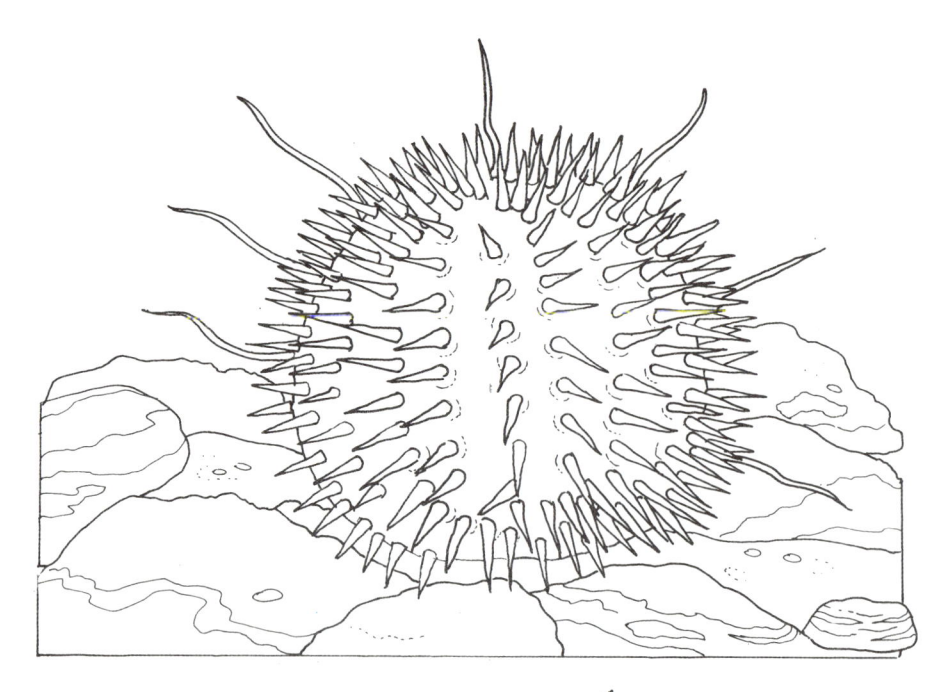

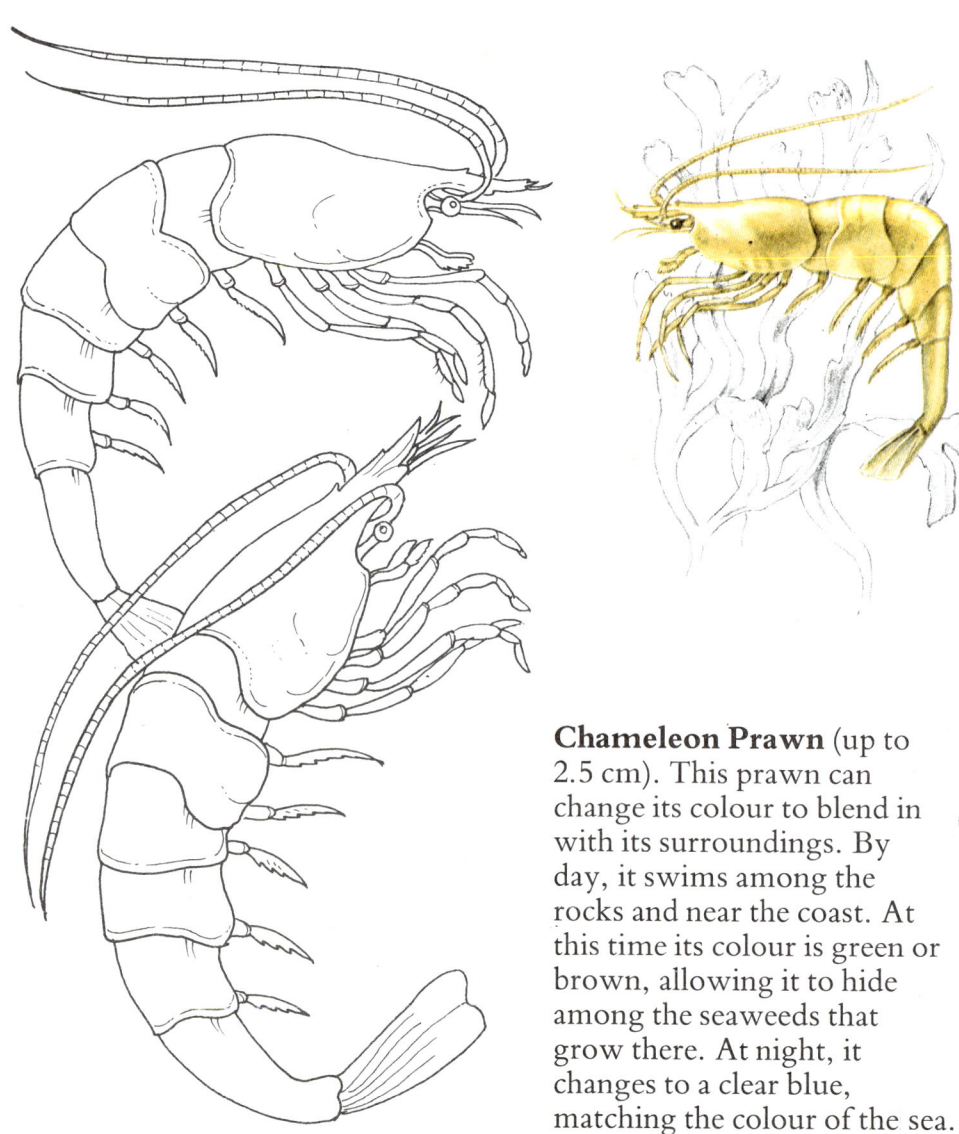

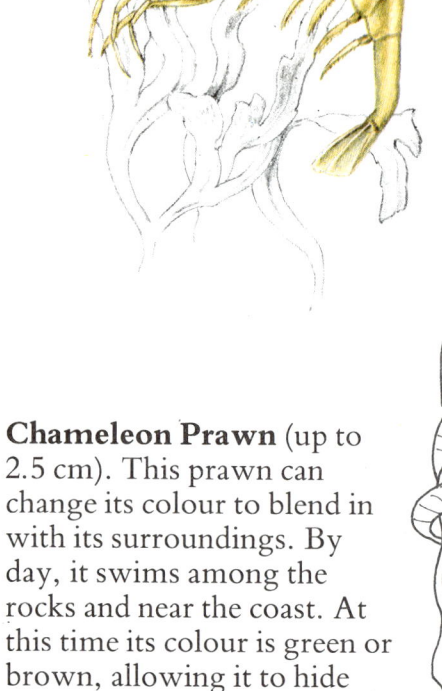

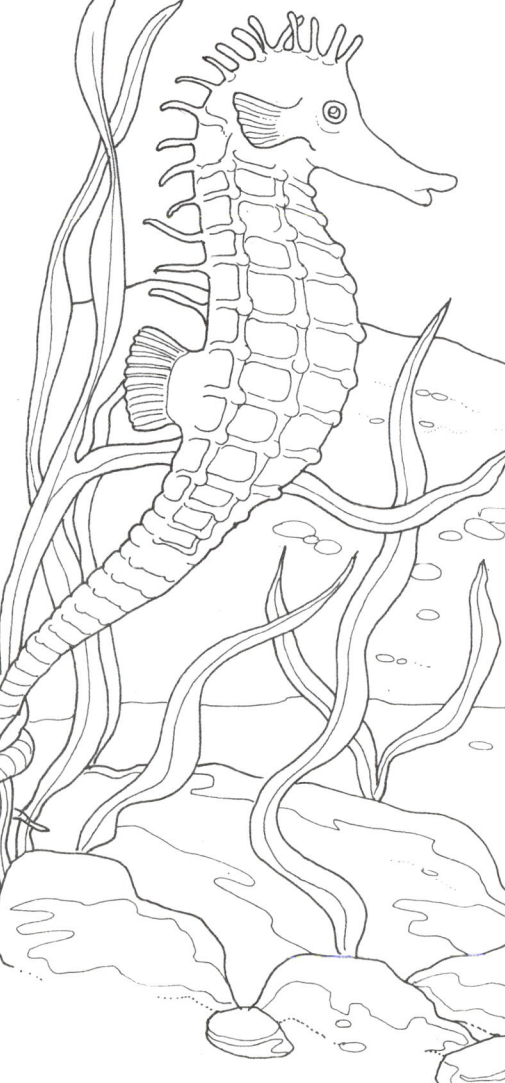

Chameleon Prawn (up to 2.5 cm). This prawn can change its colour to blend in with its surroundings. By day, it swims among the rocks and near the coast. At this time its colour is green or brown, allowing it to hide among the seaweeds that grow there. At night, it changes to a clear blue, matching the colour of the sea.

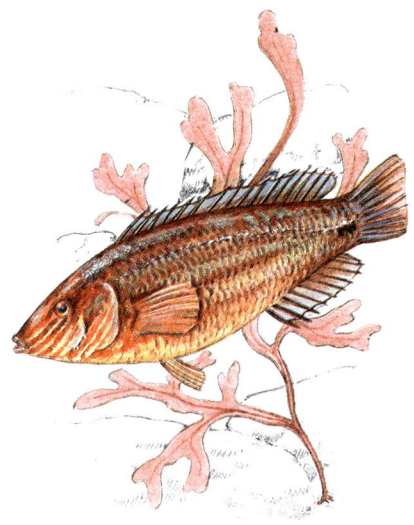

Seahorse (up to 15 cm). This unusual animal lives among seaweeds close to the shore. To feed, it twirls its long tail around a piece of weed, and reaches out with its snout to catch the tiny plants and animals that drift its way.

Corkwing Wrasse (up to 20 cm). With its red back and speckled green sides, the Corkwing Wrasse is more colourful than most of the fish found in rock pools. Although its markings vary, the black spot near the tail is always a good way of spotting this fish.

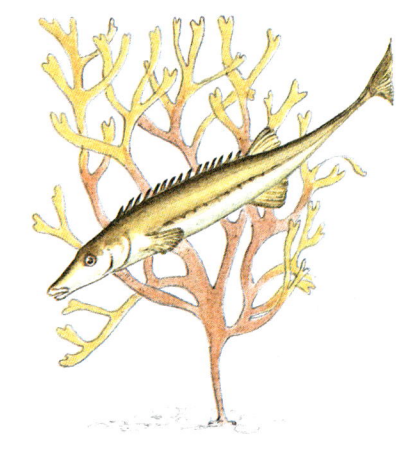

Fifteen-Spined Stickleback (up to 20 cm). This slender little fish gets its name from the sharp spines on the fin. Its silvery olive-green body can often be seen darting through the rock pools and shallow coastal waters, where it feeds on small animals that live among the seaweeds and rocks.

Kingfisher Books, Grisewood & Dempsey Ltd,
Elsley House, 24–30 Great Titchfield Street,
London W1P 7AD.
This edition published in 1990 by Kingfisher Books.
10 9 8 7 6 5 4 3
First published in 1987 under the Piccolo imprint by
Pan Books Ltd.
© Grisewood & Dempsey Ltd, 1987
All rights reserved.
ISBN 0 86272 592 5
Text written by: Meg Sanders
Editor: Deri Robins
Designer: Ben White
Illustrated by: Hayward Artists
Phototypeset by Tradespools Ltd, Frome, Somerset
Printed in Spain